Soccer File

RULES of the GAME

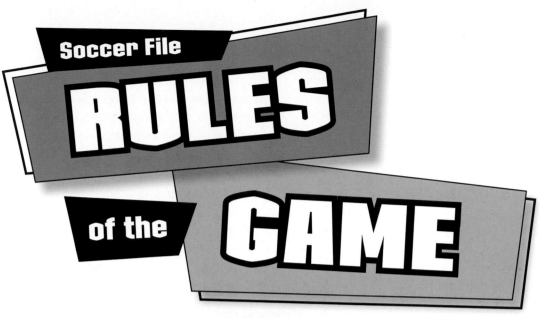

by James Nixon

Photography by Bobby Humphrey

Smart Apple Media

Published by Smart Apple Media
P.O. Box 3263, Mankato, Minnesota 56002

Printed in the United States of America at Corporate
Graphics, in North Mankato, Minnesota.

Published by arrangement with the Watts Publishing
Group Ltd., London.

Library of Congress Cataloging-in-Publication Data
Nixon, James, 1982-
  Rules of the game / James Nixon ; photography by
Bobby Humphrey.
    p. cm. -- (Soccer file)
  Includes index.
  ISBN 978-1-59920-529-8 (library binding)
  1. Soccer--Rules--Juvenile literature. I. Humphrey,
Bobby. II. Title.
  GV943.4.N58 2012
  796.334--dc22
                                        2010041760

Planning and production by
Discovery Books Limited
Editor: James Nixon
Design: Blink Media

The author, packager, and publisher would like to thank
the children of Farsley Celtic Junior Football Club for
their participation in this book.

1020
2-2011

9 8 7 6 5 4 3 2 1

Photo acknowledgements:
Getty Images: pp. 5 top (Laurence Griffiths), 8 (Alex
Grimm/Bongarts), 11 (Bongarts), 13 bottom (Andrew
Yates/AFP), 21 top (Nicholas Kahm/AFP), 22 bottom
(Daniel Garcia/AFP), 23 bottom (Vladimir Rys/
Bongarts), 28 top-right (AFP); Istockphoto.com: p. 14
top; Shutterstock: pp. 4 (Jonathan Larsen), 5 bottom
(Lario Tus), 15 top (Shawn Pecor), 15 middle (Jonathan
Larsen), 17 left (George Green), 19 top (Brandon Parry),
21 bottom (Andreas Gradin), 22 top (George Green), 25
bottom (Sport Graphic), 26 top (Adam Gasson), 26 left
(Jonathan Larsen), 26 right (Sportsphotographer.eu), 27
left (Alvaro Alexander), 27 right (Sport Graphic),
28 top-left, bottom-left (Jonathan Larsen),
27 bottom-right (Matt Trommer), 29 left
(Laszio Szirtesi), 29 right; Wikimedia: p. 20 top.

Cover photos: Shutterstock: left (Sandro Donda), right
(Sportsphotographer.eu).

Every attempt has been made to clear copyright.
Should there be any inadvertent omission please
apply to the publisher for rectification.

Statistics on pages 28–29 are correct at the time
of going to press, but in the fast-moving world
of soccer, are subject to change.

Contents

Words that appear in **bold** are in the glossary on page 30.

The RULES of the Game

To be a good soccer player, you need to understand the rules of the game. Knowing what is and is not allowed on a soccer field can give you an edge over your opponents in games. On the other hand, not knowing the rules can be very costly for your team.

The Basics

A soccer game is played between two teams with 11 players on each side. One player on each team is the goaltender. The aim is to score more goals than the opposition. Players have 90 minutes to play and score.

The game is split into two halves of 45 minutes. After the half-time break, the teams switch ends to shoot the other way. The referee can add on time at the end of each half if time has been lost for injuries, **substitutions**, and other delays.

The Rule Book

Compared to other sports, soccer is a very simple game. The official **FIFA** rule book has just 17 sections of rules. For example, this is Rule 10 (right):

Rule 10 – The Method of Scoring

"A goal is scored when the whole of the ball passes over the goal line, between the goalposts, and under the crossbar . . . The team scoring the greater number of goals in the game is the winner."

EXPERT: Jamie Carragher

Defenders must do everything they can to stop offensive players from scoring a goal. But they must defend within the rules of the game. If they break the rules, they can give away dangerous **free kicks** or even a **penalty** to their opponents. This gives the opposition a great chance to score. Liverpool star Jamie Carragher (far right) is skillful at defending without giving away **fouls**. His determination and tackling skills win him the ball. To avoid tripping players, his timing of tackles is usually right on.

The FIELD of PLAY

The field of play is where all the action takes place. White lines mark the boundary and other parts of the field. A soccer field must be rectangular in shape, but the overall size of a field can vary.

Field Size

A field can be between 100 and 130 yards (90–120 m) long and 50 to 100 yards (45–90 m) wide. Even in the professional game, field sizes can be very different. The field of play inside Real Madrid's Bernabeu stadium is 20 feet (6 m) longer and 13 feet (4 m) wider than the field at Liverpool's Anfield ground!

50 to 100 yards (45–90 m)

100 to 130 yards (90–120 m)

❶ **Halfway line** – divides the field of play into two equal halves

❷ **Center spot** – where the game kicks off or restarts after a goal

❸ **Center circle** – This marks a distance of 10 yards (9.15 m) from the center spot. At kick-offs, you cannot enter this circle until the opponents kick off.

❹ **Penalty area** – The only part of the field where the goaltender can handle the ball; This area is sometimes called "the box."

❺ **Penalty spot** – A foul in your own penalty area usually means a penalty to your opponents. The penalty kick is taken from this spot, 12 yards (11 m) from goal.

❻ **The "D"** – marks a distance of 10 yards (9.15 m) away from the penalty spot

❼ **Six-yard box** – marks where goaltenders take their goal kicks

❽ **Sidelines** – A ball that crosses the sidelines is out of play. Play restarts from a throw-in.

❾ **Goal lines** – A ball that completely crosses this line on either side of the goal results in a goal kick or a corner kick being awarded.

❿ **Corner quadrants** – Corner kicks must be taken from on or inside this arc.

⓫ **Goals**

Goalposts

The goals are located on the center of each goal line. They are 8 yards (7.3 m) wide and 8 feet (2.4 m) high. The goalposts and crossbar must be painted white.

Starts and Restarts

To start a game or half or to restart after a goal, play begins from the center spot. At the kick-off, all players must be in their own half. The kicker must play the ball forward and cannot touch it again until it has touched another player. You could actually run up and shoot at the goal right from the kick-off!

Center circle

The EQUIPMENT

Soccer players must wear a shirt, shorts, socks, shin pads, and soccer cleats. The goaltender will also wear gloves. The uniform might seem basic, but players must choose the correct type of uniform and take care of their equipment if they want to play to their full potential.

Cleats

The most important thing is to find a pair of shoes that fit well. Soccer cleats should fit snugly to your feet and support your ankles, but you shouldn't squeeze your feet into a size too small. A good shoe is made of soft leather so you can feel the ball. It should also be flexible to help the movement of your foot.

Molds or Screw-ins

Cleats can either have molded studs or screw-in studs. **Molds** (left) give you better support on dry fields. If you wear screw-ins (above) on a hard field, you will probably get blisters. Screw-in cleats are better on muddy ground because they give you more grip. If you buy just one pair of shoes, buy a screw-in pair, which can have different lengths of cleats attached for various surfaces.

Safety Rules

Players must not wear anything that is dangerous to themselves or others. The rules ban certain sizes and shapes of cleats. The referee will check each player's shoes before a game. You must also take off any kind of jewelry. Shin pads must be worn at all levels of the game. They are made out of a light but strong plastic, and they protect your lower leg from serious injury. There are different types, so find out which is best for you.

These shin pads have padding around the ankle bone for extra protection.

Shoe Care

Nobody likes cleaning their shoes after the game, but if you don't, they can crack and become hard, and your game will suffer. Always knock off the mud after a game and clean the rest with a damp cloth. Let them dry naturally—do not put them by a heater! Stuff your shoes with newspaper so they hold their shape when you are not wearing them.

Color Clashes

The two teams must wear different-colored shirts. That is why soccer teams have home and away uniforms. The away team will use their second uniform if their normal one matches the opponents'. The goalie's shirt must also be a different color from the outfield players and referees.

The REFEREE

A soccer game cannot be played without a referee. With the help of two assistants on the sideline, it is their job to control the game.

The referee makes sure that all the players follow the rules. They blow a whistle and use hand signals to communicate their decisions to players. The referee's decision is final!

Respect the Ref

Referee

Refereeing is a very tough job. Soccer is a fast-moving game, played on a big field. Referees have to be extremely fit to keep up with the play. They do more running in a game than any of the players! Decisions have to be made in a split-second. They don't get to see a slow-motion television replay from five different angles. A referee is bound to get some decisions wrong. If this happens, accept it. Never argue with the referee, or you will be **booked**.

Timekeeping

The referee doesn't just make judgments on fouls and whether the ball was in or out of play. They are also the timekeepers. They keep an eye on their watch and stop it for injuries and other delays. The end of the game is signaled with a long blow of the whistle.

EXPERT: Roberto Rosetti

Italian Roberto Rosetti is considered by many to be the best referee in the world. More often than not, he makes the right call. Rosetti was selected to referee the 2008 European Championship Final between Spain and Germany. He can speak many different languages, which helps him communicate with players from around the world on the field and gain their respect.

Whistle

Watch

Playing Advantage

When referees spot a foul, they can choose to let the game continue. They will do this if they feel the team would rather keep playing than receive a free kick. To signal that the referee is "playing advantage," they will extend both arms out in front of their body (right). Playing advantage helps to keep the game flowing. So, remember to listen for the whistle—do not stop until you hear it.

Advantage

FOULS

If you break the rules, you can expect the referee to punish you. Depending on where your foul took place, you will concede a free kick or a penalty. There are many types of fouls you can commit, from shirt-pulling or tripping to handling the ball or wasting time.

Shirt-pulling

Fouling Opponents

Tripping

When you challenge your opponent for the ball, it must be done fairly. If you kick, trip, push, or hold your opponent, the referee will blow his whistle for a foul. You must make contact with the ball before the player as you tackle. It is no good saying you got the ball if you tackled your opponent first.

Dangerous Play

A foul can also be awarded if the referee feels your challenge was dangerous. Tackling with your cleats raised in the air (right) or **slide tackling** a player from behind will always be penalized. A two-footed challenge is also against the rules. Be warned: if you play dangerously, the referee may take matters further and send you out (see pages 14–15)!

Obstruction

A **shoulder barge**, where your arm is straight and you lean into the opponent, is a legal challenge. However, it must be within playing distance of the ball. If you **obstruct** a player going toward the ball, this is a foul.

You cannot prevent the progress of a player if you are not within playing distance of the ball.

Handball

Players must not handle the ball with their hand or any part of their arm (above). If you handball deliberately, you will concede a foul. It is often tough for a referee to decide whether the handball was deliberate or not. If you are a defender blocking a shot, the safest thing to do is to keep your hands down by your side.

Goaltender Fouls

Goaltenders can give away free kicks and penalties, too. There are extra rules for goaltenders. Goaltenders must be familiar with them. They cannot:

▸ hold on to the ball for longer than six seconds
▸ touch the ball with their hands right after releasing it
▸ touch a back pass (played with the feet) or a throw-in from a teammate with their hands
▸ handle the ball outside their own penalty area

13

CARD Offenses

Some fouls and offenses are so serious that the referee will hand out extra punishment. A yellow card "cautions" a player about their behavior. If the referee shows a red card, you are sent off the field and you are out of the game. A player who is red carded has really let the team down. The team has to play the rest of the game with only ten players (or fewer if someone else has already been sent out).

Bookings

A yellow card is also known as a "booking." This is because the referee takes your name and shirt number and makes a note of the yellow card in their notebook. If you receive two yellow cards in a game, it means a red card, and you are sent out.

The offenses below will result in a yellow card:

- a bad, reckless, or deliberate foul
- persistent fouling (the referee may speak to you and give a verbal warning before showing yellow)
- wasting time, such as delaying the restart of play
- failing to retreat 10 yards (9.15 m) from a free kick or corner
- diving
- arguing with the referee, known as **dissent**
- professionals can be booked for over-the-top goal celebrations, such as removing their shirt, jumping into the crowd, or pulling out the corner flag

Gentleman Jim

Between 1946 and 1965, defender Jimmy Dickinson played 893 games for England and Portsmouth, and incredibly, did not get booked once! He earned himself the nickname "Gentleman Jim."

Bans and Fines

Getting booked or sent out doesn't just land you in trouble on the field. If you get a red card, you will also get a **suspension**. This means you are banned from playing for a certain number of games. Professional players are also charged a fine if they are carded.

Seeing Red

For the most extreme offenses, you will immediately be shown a red card. There is no excuse for being sent out. Your teammates, your fans, and your coach will be furious with you.

Handball

Red-card offenses include:
- a dangerous tackle (e.g. two-footed, high)
- violent conduct, such as punching and kicking (never raise your hands to an opponent or the referee)
- spitting at an opponent
- using insulting language or gestures
- fouling to prevent a clear goal scoring opportunity (e.g. handling the ball on your goal line (left) or tripping an opponent who is through on goal)

OFFSIDE

The offside rule, designed to stop forwards from goal-hanging, is probably the most difficult rule to understand. It is also a rule that causes much debate and controversy.

The referee must judge if the player in an offside position is interfering with play. There is a difference between being in an offside position and committing an offside offense.

Offside Position

It is not an offense to be in an offside position, but you will be flagged offside if a teammate passes to you.

▸ You are in an offside position if you are ahead of every opponent on the field except one (usually the goaltender).

▸ To be in an onside position, you need two opponents (including goaltender) between you and the goal.

▸ If you are level with the last defender, you are onside. You can be caught offside if any part of your body besides your arms is ahead of the defender.

Here, any offense player between the black dotted line and the goal is in an offside position. (To be onside, you need two opponents between you and the goal.)

Defenders

Forward

Goaltender

Offside Flag

The flag will be raised by the assistant referee if you are in an offside position at the exact moment the ball was passed to you (1). Even if the ball is not passed directly to you, you can still be offside. You will be flagged offside if you are interfering with play or gaining an advantage by being in an offside position. Interfering with play can be standing in the goaltender's line of vision (2) or distracting a defender. You are gaining an advantage if a shot or pass finds its way to you via a **deflection**, such as a rebound off the goalie (3).

Not Offside

You cannot be offside:
▸ if your teammate's pass to you was sideways or backward
▸ from a throw-in or goal kick
▸ in your own half of the field
▸ if you do not interfere with play

EXPERT: Samuel Eto'o

Forwards have to be cunning if they want to break through a defense without being offside. Samuel Eto'o, the star striker from Cameroon, is an expert at this. To stay onside, he delays his run until the second the pass is played. His speed then takes him away from the defenders. This helped him score over 100 goals in just five seasons at Barcelona, Spain.

ASSISTANT Referees

It would be impossible for a referee to run a game all by him or herself—they would need eyes in the back of their head! The referee has two assistants to help them make decisions. One assistant (left) patrols each sideline. In the past, assistant referees were called linesmen or lineswomen.

Signals

The assistant catches the referee's attention by waving a brightly-colored flag. The signal they make tells the referee their decision.

This assistant is signaling a throw-in to the team attacking the goal to his left.

This assistant has raised her flag to indicate an offside in the middle of the field. She would point the flag down if the offside took place on her side of the field and point it up if the offside was on the far side of the field.

Duties

The assistant referee's duties are:
► to indicate the ball out of play for a throw-in, goal, corner, or goal kick
► to decide which team has pushed the ball out of play
► to flag for fouls that happen near them
► to judge offside decisions. The referee relies on the assistant to make offside calls because they have the perfect view across the field. But it is still not easy to get the decision right. They have to somehow keep an eye on the ball as it is kicked and the forward at the same time.

Respect the assistants and do not argue with their decisions.

Final Say

The assistant referee can alert the referee of a foul that they have not seen, but the referee has the final say. They can overturn any decision the assistant makes if they wish.

It is not always easy for an assistant to judge if the ball has crossed the line for a goal.

Goal-Line Technology

Assistant referees also have the tricky job of trying to see if the ball has crossed the goal line for a goal. The entire ball has to cross the line. As they are standing at the side of the field, this is not always easy to see, especially if players are blocking their view. In the future, professional leagues may decide to let referees call for a video replay, which is watched by an assistant at the side of the field. Other pieces of goal-line technology are also being developed. One idea is to use a microchip built into the soccer ball. When the ball crosses the line, the microchip would send a beeping signal into the earpiece of the referee. This would tell them that a goal has been scored.

Fourth Official

At professional games, there is now a fourth official to help the referee. They signal to a referee when a team wants to make a substitution. They do this with an electronic board. The board is also used to show the crowd and players how much **stoppage time** the referee has added on.

OUT of PLAY

When the entire ball crosses the outside lines of the field, the ball is out of play and play needs to be restarted. Even if the ball curves over the line and back onto the field again, the ball is out of play. A goal kick, corner, or throw-in will be awarded depending on where the ball went out and who last touched it.

Throw-In

If the ball crosses the sidelines, a throw-in is given to the team who did not touch the ball out. This is taken from where the ball crossed the line. Here is how you should throw-in:

▸ Using both hands, spread your fingers behind the ball so your thumbs are nearly touching (1).
▸ Bring the ball forward from behind and over your head (2).
▸ Keep a part of both feet on the ground, on or behind the sideline.
▸ Follow through with your hands and fingers to direct the flight of the ball (3).

Foul Throws

You must throw-in correctly. If you don't, the referee will award a throw-in to the other side. Foul throws include lifting a foot off the ground, stepping over the sideline, and not bringing the ball back behind your head (right). You cannot score from a throw-in and the goaltender cannot handle a throw from a teammate.

EXPERT: Cat Whitehill

Most teams have a throw-in expert who can launch long, accurate throws. Cat Whitehill does this job for the United States' women's team. She takes a couple of quick steps toward the sideline, and with a leading leg in front of the other, she arches her back back and thrusts forward. A long throw is a very useful weapon. It can wreak havoc in the opposition's penalty box.

Goal Kick

When the forwards knock the ball over the goal line to the sides of the goal, the defense is awarded a goal kick. The goal kick can be taken by any player from any point inside the six-yard box (right), but the kick must leave the penalty area before any player can touch it.

Corner

If the defenders knock the ball across their own goal line (to the sides of the goal), it is a corner kick. This is taken in the quadrant from the side of the field the ball left. Once the kick is taken, another player must touch it before the kicker can touch it again. If the corner-taker touches it twice, the opposition receives an **indirect free kick** (see pages 22–23).

FREE KICKS

There are two types of free kicks depending on the type of foul. They can be direct or indirect. A direct free kick can be shot straight into the net. An indirect free kick has to touch another player before a goal can be scored. Try to avoid giving away free kicks around the penalty area. They give the opposition a chance to shoot at the goal or cross into the box.

Ref's Signals

The referee points forward with a raised arm to show the direction in which a direct free kick is awarded.

To indicate an indirect free kick, the referee raises his hand right above his head.

Stand Back

A free kick is taken from the place where the foul was committed. The defending side must retreat and stand 10 yards (9.15 m) away from the free kick. You cannot move forward to block the free kick until the ball is struck. If you do, the referee will order a repeat, and you will be booked. As with a corner kick, the kicker can only touch it once before it touches another player.

10 yards

Direct or Indirect

Most offenses, such as a trip or a handball, result in a direct free kick. Indirect free kicks are awarded for:

▸ blocking an opponent not within playing distance of the ball

▸ dangerous play, such as a challenge with a high foot

▸ taking two touches when taking a corner, throw-in, free kick, or kick-off

▸ the goaltender handling a back pass

Goalmouth Scramble

Indirect free kicks inside the opposition's penalty area can be bizarre. The defenders will often cram themselves on the goal line between the posts. As an offensive player, you can shoot on goal and hope for a deflection on the way, or you can tap it sideways for a teammate to shoot (below)—but beware: the mass of defenders will charge at you as soon as the free kick is taken, so you have to be quick.

No Goal

If you score direct from an indirect free kick, it will not count! Instead, the opposition will be awarded a goal kick.

PENALTIES

To give away a penalty is one of the worst mistakes you can make as a soccer player. For the opposition, it is the perfect chance to score. A penalty kick can be the difference between winning and losing a game. A foul that would normally be a direct free kick is a penalty if it happens inside your penalty box.

Paying the Penalty

What makes a penalty such a good chance to score? For a start, the kick is taken from a spot that is only 12 yards (11 m) away from the goal. The penalty-taker has only the goaltender to beat (right). No other player can interfere until the ball has been struck. The goalie has to stay on their line until the ball is kicked. If they move off their line too soon to save it, the kick will be repeated.

Keep Out!

All the other players on the field must stay behind the penalty spot and keep out of the penalty box and "D" until the kick is taken. You should be on your toes and rush in when the ball is struck. There may be the chance of a rebound. But, the referee can order a redo if any player enters the area too soon.

Rebounds

Once the penalty is taken, the kicker cannot touch it again until it has touched another player. So, if your penalty rebounds off the post or crossbar, leave it alone—but be ready for a rebound off the goalie. You may get a second chance to put it in the net.

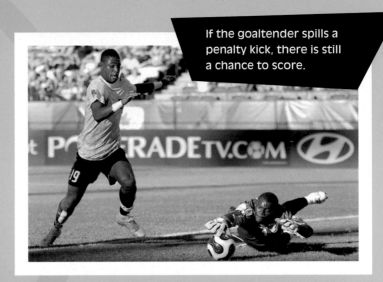

If the goaltender spills a penalty kick, there is still a chance to score.

The Goalie's View

The chances of you saving a penalty are small, but if you do pull it off, you will be a hero. You can't move off your line before the ball is kicked, but you can move along it. Some goalies bounce up and down in an attempt to throw the striker off. It is not possible to react in time to a well-placed shot to the corner. However, you can try to guess which way the ball will go (above). Try to watch the kicker carefully and dive just before the ball is struck. As you dive sideways, stretch and spread yourself out.

Shoot-outs

Unlike a league game, a **cup tie** cannot be drawn. If a replay and **overtime** cannot produce a winner, the game will be decided by a dramatic penalty shoot-out. Five players on each side take a penalty kick. If the scores are still tied, it is then **sudden death**. An extra player from each team steps up, and this continues until there is a winner.

FAIR Play

Along with the rules of the game, the world soccer organization (FIFA) has a "code of conduct." This is a list of ways in which soccer players should behave on and off the field. The code is known as the Fair Play Program. Each rule is based on respect—for the rules, officials, and opponents.

Before each professional game, players shake hands with the officials and the opposition.

The Code

▸ Observe the rules of the game.
▸ Do not cheat. Pretending to be fouled is unacceptable. You will be booked.
▸ Play fair. If the ball is kicked out of play by your opponents because a player is badly injured, make sure you return the ball to them for the restart.
▸ Play to win, but accept defeat properly. Shake hands with the referee and opposition at the end of the game (right).
▸ Respect everyone involved in the game. Do not act violently or aggressively to opponents or referees. Remember: the referee's decision is final!

Banned!

Not playing with sportsmanlike conduct can land a professional player in trouble. A dive to con the referee or a stomp on a player's leg may go unnoticed on the field. However, the television cameras see everything. The player can expect to be banned and fined for their actions. A suspension can last many months if the offense is serious.

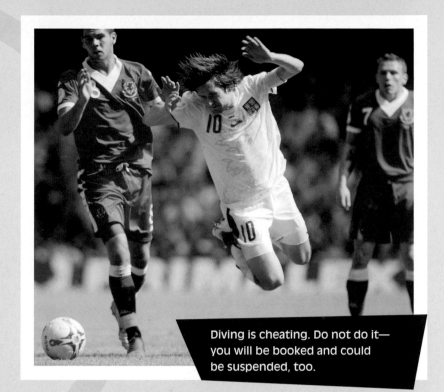

Diving is cheating. Do not do it—you will be booked and could be suspended, too.

Respect Campaign

An English soccer association has launched a campaign to make sure referees are treated properly. This is aimed at soccer players at all levels of the game. On average, 7,000 referees are quitting soccer every year because of the abuse they receive from players and spectators. Do not confront and **harass** the referee—accept their decisions. Without referees there would be no soccer games, so give the ref respect.

Fair Play Award

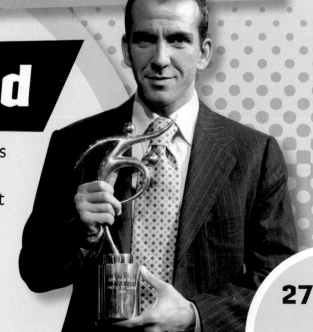

The Fair Play Award is occasionally given to players or teams. Italian striker Paulo Di Canio (right) was a past winner of the award for his special moment of **sportsmanship**. He could have scored past an injured goaltender lying on the ground. Instead, he picked up the ball and stopped the game.

The Coaches

The head of a soccer team is known as the coach. More pressure falls on their shoulders than any other person on the team. If results are going badly, it is the coach who gets the blame. The importance of a good coach, who can motivate the players and choose the correct lineup and tactics, is huge. Coaches will try to use the rules of the game to their team's advantage.

Coach Frank Rijkaard makes one of his three permitted substitutions in an attempt to swing the game in his team's favor.

On the Training Ground

During the week, coaches will prepare their teams for the next game. They will work on specific tactics. For example, they may work with the defense to use an **offside trap**. They will also instruct the players on how they should defend set pieces, such as corners and free kicks.

Substitutes

Once the team talk is over and the game has kicked off, it is out of the coach's hands—or is it? The coach can influence a game by making substitutions or changing tactics or formation. In most competitions, the rules allow up to three substitutions in a game. The substitution can only be made once the referee is ready. A substitute with fresh legs can have a big impact on a game. Once a player is substituted, they cannot be used again.

Top Coaches

Jose Mourinho

Nation: Portugal **D.O.B:** 1.26.63

CLUB RECORD

TEAM	FROM	TO	G	W	D	L	WIN %
BENFICA	SEPTEMBER 20, 2000	DECEMBER 5, 2000	11	6	3	2	54.55
LEIRIA	JANUARY 2001	JANUARY 20, 2002	31	17	10	4	54.84
PORTO	JANUARY 23, 2002	MAY 26, 2004	123	87	21	15	70.73
CHELSEA	JUNE 2, 2004	SEPTEMBER 20, 2007	185	131	36	18	70.81
INTER MILAN	JUNE 2, 2008	MAY 28, 2010	108	67	26	15	62.04
REAL MADRID	MAY 31, 2010	PRESENT	33	26	25	2	77.42

Honors: Portuguese League 2003, 2004; Portuguese Cup 2003; UEFA Cup 2003; Champions League 2004, 2010; Premier League 2005, 2006; FA Cup 2007; Italian League 2009, 2010; Italian Cup 2010

Frank Rijkaard

Nation: Netherlands **D.O.B:** 9.30.62

CLUB RECORD

TEAM	FROM	TO	G	W	D	L	WIN %
NETHERLANDS	1998	2000	22	8	12	2	36.36
SPARTA ROTTERDAM	2001	2002	34	4	18	12	11.76
BARCELONA	JULY 2003	MAY 2008	273	160	63	50	58.61
GALATASARAY	JUNE 2009	OCTOBER 2010	67	37	15	15	55.22

Honors: Spanish League 2005, 2006; Champions League 2006

Arsene Wenger

Nation: France **D.O.B:** 10.22.49

CLUB RECORD

TEAM	FROM	TO	G	W	D	L	WIN %
NANCY	1984	1987	114	33	30	51	28.95
AS MONACO	1987	1995	266	130	53	83	48.87
NAGOYA GRAMPUS EIGHT	1995	1996	56	38	0*	18	67.86
ARSENAL	SEPTEMBER 30, 1996	PRESENT	818	471	196	151	57.58

*Nagoya Grampus Eight games were not allowed to end in a draw. Matches were decided by extra time and penalties.

Honors: French League 1979; French Cup 1991; Japanese Cup 1996; Japanese League 1996; Premier League 1998, 2002, 2004; FA Cup 1998, 2002, 2003, 2005

Carlo Ancelotti

Nation: Italy **D.O.B:** 6.10.59

CLUB RECORD

TEAM	FROM	TO	G	W	D	L	WIN %
REGGIANA	1995	1996	38	16	13	9	42.11
PARMA	1996	1998	102	48	31	23	47.06
JUVENTUS	1999	2001	114	63	18	33	55.26
AC MILAN	NOVEMBER 6, 2001	MAY 31, 2009	413	234	100	79	56.66
CHELSEA	JULY 1, 2009	PRESENT	88	57	14	17	64.77

Honors: Italian Cup 2003; Italian League 2004; Champions League 2003, 2007; Premier League 2010; FA Cup 2010

Alex Ferguson

Nation: Scotland **D.O.B:** 12.31.41

CLUB RECORD

TEAM	FROM	TO	G	W	D	L	WIN %
EAST STIRLINGSHIRE	JUNE 1, 1974	OCTOBER 20, 1974	17	10	2	6	52.94
ST. MIRREN	OCTOBER 21, 1974	MAY 31, 1978	169	74	41	54	43.79
ABERDEEN	AUGUST 1, 1978	NOVEMBER 5, 1986	459	272	105	82	59.26
SCOTLAND	SEPTEMBER 10, 1985	JUNE 13,1986	10	3	4	3	30.00
MANCHESTER UNITED	NOVEMBER 6, 1986	PRESENT	1,366	807	319	240	59.08

Honors: Scottish League 1980, 1984, 1985; Scottish Cup 1982, 1983, 1984, 1986; Premier League 1993, 1994, 1996, 1997, 1999, 2000, 2001, 2003, 2007, 2008, 2009; FA Cup 1990, 1994, 1996, 1999, 2004; Champions League 1999, 2008

Silvia Neid

Nation: Germany **D.O.B:** 5.2.64

CLUB RECORD

TEAM	FROM	TO	G	W	D	L	WIN %
GERMANY	2005	PRESENT	76	54	10	12	71.05

Honors: World Cup 2007; European Championships 2009

Statistics in this book are correct at the time of going to press, but in the fast-moving world of soccer are subject to change.

Glossary

booked shown a yellow card by the referee; Get two yellow cards in a game, and you will be sent out.

cup tie a game in a competition in which teams are eliminated until there is one winner

deflection when the ball hits a player and veers off in a different direction

dissent arguing with the referee

FIFA the International Federation of Association Football, which sets rules and organizes professional soccer competition

foul an action that breaks the rules of the game, such as tripping, pushing, handball, etc.

free kick a kick of the ball awarded to a side because of a foul by the opposition

goal-hanging spending most of your time near the opponent's goal in the hope of scoring easy goals

harass behave aggressively toward someone

indirect free kick a free kick (awarded for certain fouls) that cannot be struck directly into the goal

molds plastic studs that are molded to the sole of a soccer cleat and cannot be removed

obstruct deliberately block a player's movement with your body

offside a position on the field where the ball cannot be passed to you; To be onside, you must have two opponents between you and the opponent's goal.

offside trap a tactic that a team's defense uses to catch an opponent offside

overtime an extra 30 minutes added to a tied game, split into two halves, each lasting 15 minutes

penalty a shot from the penalty spot (12 yards/11 m from goal) with just the goaltender to beat; It is awarded to the offense when the defending side has fouled in their own penalty area.

shoulder barge a lean of the body into your opponent to legally push them off the ball

slide tackling sliding the body feet-forward to take the ball from the player in possession

sportsmanship showing fair play to your opponents

stoppage time time added on to the end of each half of a soccer game for time lost due to injuries and substitutions

substitution when a player is taken off the field by the coach and replaced by someone else

sudden death where a penalty shoot-out continues until one side misses and the other scores to decide the game

suspension a player with a suspension Is prevented from playing for a certain period of time

tactics the plans and ideas used by a team to gain an edge over the opposing team

Further Information

Books

Defender by Antony Lishak (Sea-to-Sea Publications, 2008)

Eyewitness: Soccer by Hugh Hornby (DK Publishing, 2010)

Goalkeeper by Clive Gifford (Sea-to-Sea Publications, 2008)

Soccer by the Numbers by Colleen Dolphin (ABDO Publishing, 2010)

Soccer: How It Works by Suzanne Bazemore (Capstone Press, 2010)

Web Sites

www.ussoccer.com/
On this site, you can read about and watch the nation's latest soccer news, check tournament schedules, and even buy tickets!

www.soccer-training-info.com
Learn how to perfect your skills, plus study soccer strategy.

www.soccerxpert.com
A site all about playing soccer and improving your game

www.fifa.com/worldfootball/lawsofthegame.html
The official rules of the game for professional soccer, as decided by the International Federation of Association Football.

Note to parents and teachers: Every effort has been made by the publishers to ensure that these web sites are suitable for children, that they are of the highest educational value, and that they contain no inappropriate or offensive material. However, because of the nature of the Internet, it is impossible to guarantee that the contents of these sites will not be altered. We strongly advise that Internet access is supervised by a responsible adult.

Index